So you re~~a~~

LATIN
BOOK 1

ANSWER BOOK

Gresham Books Ltd
The Carriage House
Ningwood Manor
Ningwood
Isle of Wight
PO30 4NJ

First published in 1999 by Galore Park Publishing.
This edition published by Gresham Books in 2019.

ISBN 978-0-946095-66-7

Also available in the So You Really Want to Learn Latin series:

So you really want to learn Latin Book I	ISBN 978-0-946095-63-6
So you really want to learn Latin Book II	ISBN 978-0-946095-64-3
• Book II Answer Book	ISBN 978-0-946095-67-4
So you really want to learn Latin Book III	ISBN 978-0-946095-65-0
• Book III Answer Book	ISBN 978-0-946095-68-1

CONTENTS

INTRODUCTION

The answers which follow have been compiled with a view to providing users of *So you really want to learn Latin Book I* with an easy to use reference against which to check their work. The answers are in no way meant to be definitive and variations may of course be allowed, in particular with regard to word order and use of vocabulary. In the early exercises, numerous possibilities are listed (e.g. **amat** = He/she/it loves/is loving/does love), but this policy is not maintained throughout, and generally only one translation is given where a number of possibilities would be allowable. This is particularly true of verbs in the imperfect and perfect tenses, where for example **amāvit** could mean he/she has loved or loved, and **amābat** could mean he/she was loving, used to love, did love or loved, depending on the context. Please note that the answers refer to the edition of *So you really want to learn Latin* republished in 2019, which contains a very few alterations to exercises in the previously published edition.

P.S. You can now follow the course on YouTube. See back cover for details.

CHAPTER 1

Exercise 1.1

1.	vocō	I call	3.	festīnō	I hurry
	vocās	You call		festīnās	You hurry
	vocat	He/she/it calls		festīnat	He/she/it hurries
	vocāmus	We call		festīnāmus	We hurry
	vocātis	You call		festīnātis	You hurry
	vocant	They call		festīnant	They hurry
2.	nāvigō	I sail	4.	labōrō	I work
	nāvigās	You sail		labōrās	You work
	nāvigat	He/she/it sails		labōrat	He/she/it works
	nāvigāmus	We sail		labōrāmus	We work
	nāvigātis	You sail		labōrātis	You work
	nāvigant	They sail		labōrant	They work

Exercise 1.2

1. amō
2. nāvigās
3. festīnant
4. labōrat
5. vocat
6. amātis
7. cantāmus
8. nāvigat
9. aedificātis
10. cantat

Exercise 1.3

1. He/she/it sings/is singing/does sing
2. You (sing.) love/are loving/do love (or like)
3. You (sing.) sail/are sailing/do sail
4. You (pl.) call/are calling/do call
5. They build/are building/do build
6. You (pl.) hurry/are hurrying/do hurry
7. You (sing.) hurry/are hurrying/do hurry
8. I build/am building/do build
9. You (sing.) work/are working/do work
10. He/she/it calls/is calling/does call

Exercise 1.4

1. aedificāmus
2. cantant
3. festīnat
4. nāvigant
5. labōrāmus
6. amō
7. vocātis
8. nāvigat
9. vocāmus
10. festīnās

So you really want to learn Latin...

Exercise 1.5
1. aedificābō
2. aedificābunt
3. cantābis
4. nāvigābit
5. festīnābit
6. festīnābimus
7. amābitis
8. vocābunt
9. labōrābitis
10. vocābimus

Exercise 1.6
1. They will hurry
2. You (pl.) work/are working/do work
3. You (pl.) build/are building/do build
4. You (pl.) will love/like
5. He/she/it will call
6. They work/are working/do work
7. You (sing.) will sail
8. They will sing
9. You (sing.) sing/are singing/do sing
10. You (pl.) will build

Exercise 1.7
1. aedificābam
2. labōrābant
3. nāvigābās
4. aedificābat
5. cantābat
6. festīnābātis
7. festīnābāmus
8. vocābāmus
9. vocābātis
10. cantābant

Exercise 1.8
1. They were asking/used to ask
2. He/she/it was not overcoming/used not to overcome
3. You (sing.) will watch
4. You (pl.) were hurrying/used to hurry and I was preparing/used to prepare
5. You (pl.) were not calling/used not to call
6. They were fighting/used to fight and were overcoming/used to overcome
7. He/she/it fights/is fighting but we work/are working
8. He/she/it was calling/used to call and he/she/it was hurrying/used to hurry
9. You (sing.) were fighting/used to fight but I was overcoming/used to overcome
10. We shall not fight

Book 1 Answers

4

Exercise 1.9

1. vocō, vocāre, vocāvī, vocātum = I call, to call, I have called, in order to call
2. aedificō, aedificāre, aedificāvī, aedificātum = I build, to build, I have built, in order to build
3. cantō, cantāre, cantāvī, cantātum = I sing, to sing, I have sung, in order to sing
4. exspectō, exspectāre, exspectāvī, exspectātum = I wait for, to wait for, I have waited for, in order to wait for

Exercise 1.10

1. nāvigāvī
2. vocāvistī
3. aedificāvistī
4. labōrāvērunt
5. festīnāvit
6. aedificāvī
7. nōn exspectāvimus
8. nāvigāvit
9. labōrāvistis
10. rogāvimus

Exercise 1.11

1. We have sailed
2. To love/like
3. He/she/it has called
4. They have worked
5. You (pl.) have hurried
6. They have sailed
7. I have worked and built
8. I have not called
9. You (sing.) have not built
10. To hurry

Exercise 1.12

1. aedificāmus
2. labōrāre
3. festīnābis
4. nāvigābāmus
5. vocābant
6. amābitis
7. pugnāre
8. vocāvistī
9. nōn aedificābō
10. nōn labōrat

Exercise 1.13

1. labōrō = I work. A laboratory is a place in which one works.
2. nāvigō = I sail. To navigate is to plot a course while sailing.
3. vocō = I call. A vocation is a calling.
4. exspectō = I wait for. To expect is to wait for.

Exercise 1.14

1. aedificat
2. pugnābant
3. cantābimus
4. nāvigāvistis
5. nōn spectābant
6. nōn pugnat
7. amābās
8. nōn spectābimus
9. nāvigāvit
10. exspectābam

So you really want to learn Latin...

Exercise 1.15
1. They build/are building/do build
2. To hurry
3. We were not fighting/used not to fight
4. You (pl.) will sail
5. I was singing/used to sing but you (sing.) were working/used to work
6. You (pl.) were sailing/used to sail
7. He/she/it has fought and has overcome
8. You (pl.) watch/are watching/do watch
9. You (sing.) will build
10. You (pl.) have sailed

Exercise 1.16
1. labōrō, labōrāre, labōrāvī, labōrātum = I work
2. parō, parāre, parāvī, parātum = I prepare
3. cantō, cantāre, cantāvī, cantātum = I sing
4. aedificō, aedificāre, aedificāvī, aedificātum = I build

Exercise 1.17
1. They have loved/liked
2. He/she/it will love/like
3. You love/are loving/do love (like)
4. He/she/it was loving/used to love (like)
5. We shall love/like
6. He/she/it has loved/liked
7. You (sing.) were loving/used to love (like)
8. You (pl.) have loved/liked

Exercise 1.18
1. Romulus founded Rome in 753 B.C.
2. The story of Rome's foundation dates back to the time of the Trojan War.
3. Agamemnon, the leader of the Greek army, captured Troy in c. 1250 B.C.
4. Most of the inhabitants of Troy were either killed or led into slavery.
5. Aeneas was the son of the goddess Venus and the Trojan prince Anchises.
6. Aeneas left Troy because he was ordered to do so.
7. He was ordered to take the household gods with him.
8. He took (among others) his father Anchises and his son Ascanius (or Iulus).
9. Aeneas eventually arrived in Italy.
10. On arriving in Italy, Aeneas fought with Turnus.
11. Aeneas fought for the hand of Lavinia, the daughter of King Latinus.
12. Aeneas built the city of Lavinium.
13. Ascanius left Lavinium and founded his own city, Alba Longa.
14. Many generations later, Romulus was born in Alba Longa.

Book 1 Answers

CHAPTER 2

Exercise 2.1

1. incola
   incola
   incolam
   incolae
   incolae
   incolā

   incolae
   incolae
   incolās
   incolārum
   incolīs
   incolīs

2. fābula
   fābula
   fābulam
   fābulae
   fābulae
   fābulā

   fābulae
   fābulae
   fābulās
   fābulārum
   fābulīs
   fābulīs

3. nauta
   nauta
   nautam
   nautae
   nautae
   nautā

   nautae
   nautae
   nautās
   nautārum
   nautīs
   nautīs

4. rēgīna
   rēgīna
   rēgīnam
   rēgīnae
   rēgīnae
   rēgīnā

   rēgīnae
   rēgīnae
   rēgīnās
   rēgīnārum
   rēgīnīs
   rēgīnīs

Exercise 2.2

1. agricolae
2. nautae
3. fābulae
4. fābulā
5. agricolae
6. agricolae
7. agricolam
8. nautīs
9. nauta
10. agricolārum

Exercise 2.3

	S	V	O
1.	The farmer loves the girl.		

	S	V	O
2.	The girls love the queen.		

	S	V	O
4.	The girls love stories.		

	S	V	O
5.	The sailors will overcome the farmers.		

So you really want to learn Latin...

	S	V	O			S	V	O
3.	The sailors love the girls.			6.	The farmers will overcome the sailors.			

Exercise 2.4
1. agricola puellam amat.
2. puellae rēgīnam amant.
3. nautae puellās amant.
4. puellae fābulās amant.
5. nautae agricolās superābunt.
6. agricolae nautās superābunt.

Exercise 2.5
1. nautae patriam amant.
2. agricola nōn labōrābat.
3. fēminae mēnsās parant.
4. nautae nōn pugnābant.
5. agricolae viam parāvērunt.
6. fēmina nōn festīnābit.
7. nautae aquam amant.
8. puella cantābat.
9. fēmina puellās vocābat.
10. fēminae cantābant.

Exercise 2.6
1. fābulās amāmus.
2. nauta fābulās amat.
3. patriam superant.
4. fēmina aquam amat.
5. nautam superāvit.
6. agricolam vocābunt.
7. mēnsam nōn parābō.
8. mēnsās parant.
9. viam aedificāvistis.
10. puellam vocāvit.

Exercise 2.7
1. nautae
2. incolās
3. īnsulae
4. fēmina
5. puellae
6. sapientiam
7. viae
8. pugnārum
9. fābula
10. fāmae

Exercise 2.8
1. fēminae sapientiam amant.
2. incolae nautās superāvērunt.
3. nautae Rōmam nōn oppugnābunt.
4. puellae labōrant.
5. agricolae sagittās parāvērunt.

Exercise 2.9
1. fēmina = woman; feminine relates to females (thus women).
2. aqua = water; aquatic relates to water.
3. fābula = story; a fable is a story.
4. labōrō = I work; if something is laborious, it involves hard work.
5. nāvigō = I sail; to navigate is to steer a boat.

Book 1 Answers

Exercise 2.10
1. The farmer loves the girl.
2. The farmer has overcome the sailors.
3. The woman was loving/used to love the girl.
4. The sailor will overcome the farmer.
5. The girls used to love the farmer.
6. The woman was not preparing the water.
7. The farmers have prepared the way; *or*
   They have prepared the way for / of the farmer
8. The sailor has prepared the arrows.
9. The sailors used to love the island; *or*
   They used to love the island of the sailor.
10. The inhabitants love fame; *or* They love the fame of the inhabitant.

Exercise 2.11
1. The inhabitants attack Rome.
2. The farmer has prepared the ground.
3. We do not love Greece.
4. The girls have prepared the table; *or*
   They have prepared the table of / for the girl.
5. You (pl.) have not prepared the arrows.
6. We shall not overcome the inhabitants.
7. He/she has prepared the way.
8. You do not love your* fatherland (*Note how Latin regularly omits possessive adjectives if they can be assumed).
9. The farmers overcome the woman.
10. The women used to love Troy.

Exercise 2.12
1. The farmer
2. The women
3. The sailor/o sailor
4. Fame/O fame
5. With/by/from the water
6. The battle
7. Of the islands
8. Of the inhabitants
9. To/for/with/by/from the arrows
10. With/by/from wisdom

Exercise 2.13
1. To sail
2. You (sing.) will build
3. But
4. They prepare
5. I shall not fight
6. They have worked
7. You (pl.) were singing
8. You (pl.) have overcome
9. I have hurried
10. He/she was loving

So you really want to learn Latin…

Exercise 2.14

1. Ascanius was the son of Aeneas.
2. He left Lavinium.
3. The name of the city he built was Alba Longa.
4. After the death of Proca, Numitor should have been king.
5. Amulius became king instead of his brother.
6. He locked Rhea Silvia up and forced her to become a Vestal Virgin.
7. He did this because Vestal Virgins were not allowed to marry. He did not wish his brother's daughter to produce an heir.
8. According to legend, the father of Romulus and Remus was the god Mars.
9. When the babies were discovered they were thrown into the River Tiber.
10. The river had been in flood and when the waters subsided the babies were washed up on the bank.
11. A she-wolf found the babies.
12. A shepherd called Faustulus rescued the babies.
13. Numitor recognised his grandsons when Remus was brought before him following a dispute over stolen sheep. When Romulus came to rescue his brother and Numitor saw the boys together, he recognised them as his grandsons.
14. Amulius was driven from the kingdom.
15. Moses in the bullrushes. To a lesser extent, Mowgli in the Jungle Book. Perhaps even Danae and Perseus.

CHAPTER 3

Exercise 3.1
1. puellae mēnsam agricolae* parant. (*Genitives may come either before or after the nouns with which they go: mēnsam agricolae and agricolae mēnsam are both equally correct.)
2. incolae fāmam Troiae amant.
3. Rōmam sagittīs nōn oppugnāmus.
4. viam incolīs parābunt.
5. mēnsam fēminae parāvit.
6. puellae, agricolae fēminīs cantant.
7. sagittae incolārum nautās superant.
8. mēnsās fēminīs parābant.
9. agricolae, patriam sagittīs nōn superābitis.
10. nautae, incolās nōn superāvistis.

Exercise 3.2
1. incolae Rōmae fāmam Graeciae amant.
2. nautae incolās patriae sagittīs superābunt.
3. agricola, incolae patriae Graeciam superāvērunt.
4. viam incolīs patriae aedificābat.
5. puellae mēnsam nautae parant.

Exercise 3.3
1. The girl was telling a story to the women.
2. The farmers were building a road for the inhabitants.
3. The inhabitants of Rome used to love the fame of Troy.
4. O sailors, you have overcome the farmers.
5. The inhabitants were preparing water for the farmers.
6. The sailors have overcome the inhabitant with arrows.
7. O farmers, you will prepare the roads and land for the inhabitants.
8. They do not love the stories of Troy and the fame of Greece.

Exercise 3.4
1. The girl was loving/used to love the farmer's stories.
2. The farmer was not loving/used not to love the story.
3. The woman has prepared the table for the farmers.
4. The girl was preparing arrows for the farmers.
5. O farmers, you will not overcome the women with arrows.
6. O girls, the farmers will not overcome the women.
7. The inhabitants of Troy have overcome the inhabitants of Italy.
8. The sailors have overcome the inhabitants of Italy.

So you really want to learn Latin...

Exercise 3.5
1. Of the farmer, to/for the farmer, the farmers (subject), o farmers
2. With/by/from wisdom
3. To/for/by/with/from the girls
4. Of the lands
5. With/by/from water
6. Of the stories
7. To/for/with/by/from the arrows
8. Of the battle, to/for the battle, the battles (subject), o battles

Exercise 3.6
1. ad īnsulam
2. per viās
3. in aquam
4. contrā incolās
5. in aquā
6. cum fēminīs
7. prope mēnsam
8. dē Troiā
9. ē patriā
10. post fābulam

Exercise 3.7
1. In/on the road
2. Against the farmers
3. Into/on to the road
4. From the country
5. With the farmer
6. Into the battle
7. Down from/concerning the table
8. Through/along the roads
9. Under water
10. Around Rome

Exercise 3.8
1. Aeneas has sailed from his country.
2. He was hurrying to Italy.
3. Aeneas fights with the inhabitants of Italy.
4. The farmers of Italy were walking around the sailors.
5. They were hurrying to the water.
6. The sailors were fighting with the farmers.
7. They were walking along the roads of their country.
8. They have prepared the tables near the water.
9. They were carrying water to the table.
10. They were telling stories to the inhabitants.

Exercise 3.9
1. agricola prope mēnsam labōrābat et puellam spectābat.
2. puella aquam portābat et mēnsam fēminīs parābat.
3. nauta sagittam portābat et ad puellam festīnābat.
4. incolās superāvit sed puellam sagittā vulnerāvit.
5. fēminae per viam festīnābant et pugnam spectābant.

Book 1 Answers

Exercise 3.10
1. The farmers were preparing the ground and building a road.
2. The inhabitants were loving the farmers and were telling stories.
3. The women do not work but tell stories to the farmers.
4. The girls were not telling stories but were watching the farmers.
5. The farmers were not working but were hurrying into the water.

Exercise 3.11
1. īnsula = island. Something that is insulated is surrounded, as an island is surrounded by water.
2. fāma = fame. Fame is the state of having a widespread positive reputation.
3. habitō = I live, inhabit. To inhabit is to live in.
4. fābula = story. If something is fabulous, it is the stuff of stories.
5. per = along, ambulō = I walk. Perambulation is walking along.
6. contrā = against. Contrary is opposed to.
7. in = in/into, vocō = I call. An invocation is a calling upon a higher power, e.g. a deity.
8. nārrō = I tell. A narration is a telling.
9. nauta = sailor. Nautical relates to the affairs of sailors and the sea.
10. patria = country/fatherland. If one is patriotic, one loves one's country.

Exercise 3.12
1. Under water
2. After the story
3. Before the battle
4. In the islands
5. With the inhabitants
6. Among/between the farmers
7. Without the arrows
8. Through/along the road
9. Concerning/down from Troy
10. Near Rome

Exercise 3.13
1. Romulus and Remus decided to build a new city after they had restored their grandfather Numitor to his rightful place on the throne of Alba Longa.
2. They thought the place where Faustulus had found them would make a good place for their city.
3. They decided to rely on augury to decide who should be king.
4. Romulus climbed the Palatine Hill.
5. Remus climbed the Aventine Hill.
6. Remus thought the omens were favourable because he saw six vultures.
7. Romulus however had seen twelve vultures.
8. Rome was called Rome after its founder, Romulus.
9. It might have been called Reme had Remus been its first king.
10. Remus was killed by his brother after jumping over the partially built city walls.

So you really want to learn Latin...

CHAPTER 4

Exercise 4.1
1. moneō, monēs, monet, monēmus, monētis, monent
2. terrēbō, terrēbis, terrēbit, terrēbimus, terrēbitis, terrēbunt
3. habēbam, habēbās, habēbat, habēbāmus, habēbātis, habēbant
4. dēbuī, dēbuistī, dēbuit, dēbuimus, dēbuistis, dēbuērunt

Exercise 4.2
1. docēbat
2. vident
3. timēbimus
4. tenēbit
5. nōn timētis
6. docēre
7. monuērunt
8. terruit
9. tenuistī
10. nōn timēmus

Exercise 4.3
1. He/she was fearing
2. They will teach
3. You (pl.) have not taught
4. He/she will warn
5. To have and to hold
6. He/she holds
7. They have warned
8. To fear
9. You (pl.) were holding
10. We shall have

Exercise 4.4
1. 2nd: maneō, manēs, manet, manēmus, manētis, manent
2. 1st: cēlō, cēlās, cēlat, cēlāmus, cēlātis, cēlant
3. 2nd: dēleō, dēlēs, dēlet, dēlēmus, dēlētis, dēlent
4. 1st: vītō, vītās, vītat, vītāmus, vītātis, vītant
5. 2nd: sedeō, sedēs, sedet, sedēmus, sedētis, sedent

Exercise 4.5

annus	dominus	locus	victōria	servus
anne	domine	loce	victōria	serve
annum	dominum	locum	victōriam	servum
annī	dominī	locī	victōriae	servī
annō	dominō	locō	victōriae	servō
annō	dominō	locō	victōriā	servō
annī	dominī	locī	victōriae	servī
annī	dominī	locī	victōriae	servī
annōs	dominōs	locōs	victōriās	servōs
annōrum	dominōrum	locōrum	victōriārum	servōrum
annīs	dominīs	locīs	victōriīs	servīs
annīs	dominīs	locīs	victōriīs	servīs

Book 1 Answers

Exercise 4.6
1. dominī
2. prope locum
3. nūntiō
4. sine dominō
5. ad locum
6. annōrum
7. cum dominō
8. circum locum
9. nūntiī
10. ad nūntium

Exercise 4.7
1. Towards the place
2. Before the victory
3. In the place
4. Among/between the inhabitants
5. Without water
6. Of the messengers
7. With the messengers
8. O lord/master
9. Around the table
10. Near the place

Exercise 4.8
1. servī dominum timent.
2. fēminae servōs docēbant.
3. dominus locum incolīs parābit.
4. servī terram dominō parāvērunt.
5. nūntiī fābulam servō nārrant.

Exercise 4.9

tēlum	dōnum	auxilium	perīculum
tēlum	dōnum	auxilium	perīculum
tēlum	dōnum	auxilium	perīculum
tēlī	dōnī	auxiliī	perīculī
tēlō	dōnō	auxiliō	perīculō
tēlō	dōnō	auxiliō	perīculō
tēla	dōna	auxilia	perīcula
tēla	dōna	auxilia	perīcula
tēla	dōna	auxilia	perīcula
tēlōrum	dōnōrum	auxiliōrum	perīculōrum
tēlīs	dōnīs	auxiliīs	perīculīs
tēlīs	dōnīs	auxiliīs	perīculīs

Exercise 4.10
1. The farmer was carrying a spear.
2. The slave will love the gift.
3. You were calling the messenger of the lord.
4. The spear of the master was wounding the slave; *or*
   The spear was wounding the slave of the master.

So you really want to learn Latin...

5. The spears of the master will wound the inhabitants.
6. The inhabitant has carried spears towards the master.
7. The sailors were holding spears near the water; *or*
   They were holding the spears of the sailor near the water.
8. We shall carry spears and gifts to the inhabitants of the island.
9. They were overcoming the inhabitants with the help of the farmers.
10. The master has warned the slaves concerning the spears.

Exercise 4.11
1. dominus patriae servōs monuit.
2. domine, perīcula bellī nōn timēmus.
3. fēmina servōs tēlō superābit.
4. domine, tēla servōrum nōn timēmus.
5. fēmina ad agricolās festīnābat.
6. agricolae dōna fēminae tenēbant.
7. fēmina, dōna ā terrā Troiae portāvimus.
8. agricolae, dōna nōn amō.
9. nautae oppidum tēlīs oppugnāvērunt.
10. auxiliō servōrum agricolae incolās superāvērunt.

Exercise 4.12
A farmer was telling a story: 'The inhabitants of Greece were fighting with the inhabitants of Troy. They did not destroy Troy. The inhabitants of Troy feared the inhabitants of Greece but they wounded the inhabitants of Greece with many arrows and spears.

I lived near Troy and I fought in the war. I had many spears and fought in the battles. But I hid my arrows under the table. The inhabitants of Greece feared arrows. The inhabitants of Greece overcame the farmers of Troy and destroyed the land. After the victory, the inhabitants of Greece were sitting near the table. I was sitting under the table with my arrows. I wounded the inhabitants and with the help of my arrows I overcame the inhabitants.'

The farmer told the story to many inhabitants of Rome. The inhabitants did not like the story.

Book 1 Answers

Exercise 4.13

fēmina dōna puellae dabat. puella fēminam nōn amābat sed dōna amābat. prope fēminam sēdit et fābulam fēminae nārrāvit.

'servus in īnsulā habitābat. aquam nōn habēbat. incolās īnsulae vocāvit sed labōrābant. per viās festīnāvit et nautam vocāvit. nauta servum spectāvit. servus nautam spectāvit. nauta aquam habēbat. aquam servō nōn dabat. servus nautam tēlō superāvit et aquam per viās portāvit.'

fēmina fābulam nōn amāvit; sed puella dōna amāvit.

Exercise 4.14
1. moneō = I warn/advise. A monitor warns or advises.
2. dēleō = I destroy. If one deletes something, one destroys it.
3. sedeō = I sit. A session is literally a sitting, e.g. a session of parliament.
4. annus = year. An annual event happens every year.
5. auxilium = help. An auxiliary engine is there to help if the main engine fails.
6. dominus = lord/master. To dominate is to achieve mastery.
7. dōnum = gift. A donation is a gift.
8. locus = place. A location is a place.
9. servus = slave. To be servile is to behave like a slave.
10. bellum = war. Bellicose means warlike.

Exercise 4.15
1. The population of Rome before the arrival of the women consisted of shepherds and criminals.
2. Romulus invited girls from neighbouring tribes to come to Rome.
3. This was unsuccessful because the girls' fathers did not wish their daughters to live with a band of criminals.
4. Romulus organised a festival because he knew that the neighbouring tribes would wish to participate in the feasting and games.
5. The festival would have involved animal sacrifices, feasting, processions, games and markets, primarily in the name of honouring the gods.
6. Most visitors came from the Sabine tribe.
7. At the given signal, Romulus's men seized the women.
8. The Sabine women would no doubt have been most alarmed, although the picture on page 44 of the text book suggests some of them relished the idea!

So you really want to learn Latin...

CHAPTER 5

Exercise 5.1
1. malōs
2. fessae
3. īrātīs
4. longī
5. magnae

Exercise 5.2

1. mēnsās bonās	6. servōrum bonōrum
2. nautam bonum*	7. bellī bonī
3. agricolam bonum*	8. domine bone
4. perīculum bonum	9. dominōs bonōs
5. puellārum bonārum	10. tēlī bonī

It is a very common mistake to make the adjective simply rhyme with the noun. Agricola and nauta are both masculine, despite the fact that they go like mēnsa, and the adjectives thus have to be masculine.

Exercise 5.3

1. in perīculō magnō	6. in pugnā magnā
2. servī malī	7. cum incolīs bonīs
3. nautae bonī	8. sub mēnsīs longīs
4. ex īnsulā magnā	9. per viam longam
5. agricolae fessō	10. puellārum īrātārum

Exercise 5.4
1. The angry master has called the bad slave.
2. The tired farmers were preparing the land; *or*
   They were preparing the land of the tired farmer.
3. Many farmers were overcoming the inhabitant with long spears.
4. The bad masters do not love the tired slaves; *or*
   They do not love the tired slaves of the bad master.
5. They were overcoming the inhabitants with big spears and many arrows.

Exercise 5.5

1.		2.	
	liber		ager
	liber		ager
	librum		agrum
	librī		agrī
	librō		agrō
	librō		agrō
	librī		agrī
	librī		agrī
	librōs		agrōs
	librōrum		agrōrum
	librīs		agrīs
	librīs		agrīs

Exercise 5.6
1. The good master has called the tired boy.
2. I shall teach the boys about* the great war.
   (*Note this common meaning of dē)
3. The good boy does not love the great wars.
4. He/she has hurried into the big fields with the slaves.
5. The angry master has watched the boy and the slaves.
6. I shall not teach the bad boys.
7. The big farmer was working in the field.
8. He/she has overcome the boy and the slaves with a long spear.
9. The boy and the slaves were fighting with the bad farmer.
10. The master has not given help to the boy.

Exercise 5.7
agricola īrātus per viam ambulābat. puerum spectābat. puer fābulam fēminae nārrābat. agricola ad puerum festīnāvit et clāmāvit. 'puer, in agrō meō sedēs.' puer in terrā sedēbat. in locō manēbat sed tēlum cēlābat. 'agricola, in agrō sedēbō.' fēmina timēbat sed puer in locō manēbat. agricola īrātus per viam longam ad puerum ambulāvit sed puer agricolam superāvit.

Exercise 5.8
1. vestrī
2. nostrīs
3. miserōrum
4. meā

So you really want to learn Latin...

Exercise 5.9
1. agricola miser
2. fīlia mea
3. dōna pulchra
4. puellārum tenerārum
5. sagittīs nostrīs
6. incolae Troiae, terram pulchram spectāvimus.
7. sapientiā nostrā incolās Graeciae superāvimus.
8. nūntiōs fessōs vocābimus.
9. nautae fessī circum īnsulam pulchram nāvigant.
10. patriam nostram sagittīs et tēlīs nōn superābis/superābitis.

Exercise 5.10
1. Our masters have warned the tired girls.
2. The boys were not holding the long books; *or*
   They were not holding the long books of the boy.
3. O boys, you will carry the books to the table of the master.
4. We shall not carry the books to the big table.
5. The masters were telling stories to the girls; *or*
   They were telling the master's stories to the girls.
6. The girls loved the stories but feared the masters; *or*
   They loved the girl's stories but feared the masters.
7. The bad girl has hidden the book under the table.
8. The master waited for the beautiful girl.
9. I do not love bad girls.
10. The girls and boys walked out of the place and hurried into the fields.

Exercise 5.11
1. patriam nostram amāmus.
2. fābulās meās amant.
3. domine, librōs tuōs nōn amāmus.
4. dominī, librōs vestrōs nōn amāmus.
5. cōpiae nostrae castra magna prope aquam aedificāvērunt.
6. Rōmule, copiae tuae incolās patriae superāvērunt.
7. puellae, librōs vestrōs sub mēnsā vestrā cēlāvistis.
8. Rōmule, incolae patriae meae cōpiās tuās superāvērunt.
9. castra in agrō magnō agricolae īrātī parābimus.
10. dominōs tuōs monuistī.

Book 1 Answers

Exercise 5.12

LATIN	ENGLISH	FRENCH	SPANISH	ITALIAN
portāre	porter	porter	transportar	portare
amāre	amorous*	aimer	amar	amare
dōnum	donation	donner	don	dono
amīcus	amicable	ami	amigo	amico
annus	annual	an	año	anno

Strictly this comes from amor = love, but could be allowed here.

Exercise 5.13
1. dēlet
2. timēmus
3. cēlās
4. manēmus
5. dant
6. bellum
7. annus
8. tēla
9. auxiliō
10. dōnī
11. servī
12. in perīculō
13. post fābulās
14. cum fēminā
15. per viam
16. dē Rōmā
17. ē patriā
18. in viam
19. in aquā
20. contrā incolās

Exercise 5.14
1. Titus Tatius was king of the Sabines.
2. He was not happy because the Romans had tricked him into losing his women-folk.
3. He collected an army together and attacked Rome.
4. Tarpeia was the daughter of of one of the Roman commanders.
5. She had gone outside the walls to get water.
6. She met a group of Sabine soldiers.
7. Tarpeia admired the gold bracelets and rings which the soldiers were wearing.
8. She offered to let the soldiers into the city, despite the fact that they were the enemy.
9. The soldiers kept their promise to Tarpeia by throwing their shields, which they had in their left hands, on top of Tarpeia.
10. The moral of this story is don't be treacherous! Or don't be tempted by riches.

So you really want to learn Latin...

CHAPTER 6

Exercise 6.1
1. cadō, cadis, cadit, cadimus, caditis, cadunt
2. surgō, surgis, surgit, surgimus, surgitis, surgunt
3. clamō, clāmās, clāmat, clāmāmus, clāmātis, clāmant
4. terreō, terrēs, terret, terrēmus, terrētis, terrent

Exercise 6.2
1. cadam, cadēs, cadet, cadēmus, cadētis, cadent
2. surgam, surgēs, surget, surgēmus, surgētis, surgent
3. clāmābō, clāmābis, clāmābit, clāmābimus, clāmābitis, clāmābunt
4. terrēbō, terrēbis, terrēbit, terrēbimus, terrēbitis, terrēbunt

Exercise 6.3
1. currēbam, currēbās, currēbat, currēbāmus, currēbātis, currēbant
2. gerēbam, gerēbās, gerēbat, gerēbāmus, gerēbātis, gerēbant
3. scrībēbam, scrībēbās, scrībēbat, scrībēbāmus, scrībēbātis, scrībēbant
4. dūcēbam, dūcēbās, dūcēbat, dūcēbāmus, dūcēbātis, dūcēbant

Exercise 6.4
1. cucurrī, cucurristī, cucurrit, cucurrimus, cucurristis, cucurrērunt
2. gessī, gessistī, gessit, gessimus, gessistis, gessērunt
3. clāmāvī, clāmāvistī, clāmāvit, clāmāvimus, clāmāvistis, clāmāvērunt
4. cecidī, cecidistī, cecidit, cecidimus, cecidistis, cecidērunt
5. dūxī, dūxistī, dūxit, dūximus, dūxistis, dūxērunt

Exercise 6.5
1. Why were you walking in the fields?
2. Are you walking in the fields?
3. You will walk in the fields, won't you?
4. You haven't walked in the fields, have you?
5. Who will teach the boys?
6. Where were you working, farmers?
7. Who rules the inhabitants of the country?
8. The master will teach the boys and girls, won't he?
9. The boys and girls don't love the master, do they? *or*
   They don't love the master of the boy and girl, do they?
10. Shall we overcome the forces with arrows and spears?

Exercise 6.6

*N.B. The -ne is properly added to the word on which the force of the question falls. This will thus often require an alteration to the familiar subject-object-verb word order. In English we do this with the tone of our voice, or by using italics. E.g. 'Does the **farmer** sail the ship?' may be distinguished from 'Does the farmer **sail** the ship?'*

1. amatne agricola puellam?
2. nāvigābitne nauta ad īnsulam?
3. magisterne puerōs docēbit?
4. num magister librum cēlāvit?
5. nōnne incolās Ītaliae superābimus?
6. cūr agricola fessus in agrō manet?
7. ubi librum puellae cēlābis/cēlābitis?
8. parantne servī mēnsam dominī?
9. parāvēruntne servī aquam fēminae?
10. num Troiae cōpiae incolās superābunt?

Exercise 6.7

1. miser = wretched. Miserable means wretched or unhappy.
2. ager = field or agricola = farmer. Agriculture relates to care of the fields.
3. multus = much or many. To multiply is to increase in number.
4. cōpiae = forces / cōpia = supply. The word copious means plentiful, and is properly derived from the singular meaning of cōpia = a supply.
5. īrātus = angry. Irate means angry.
6. annus = year. An annual event happens every year.
7. dēleō = I destroy. To delete something is to destroy it.
8. dominus = master. To dominate is to achieve mastery.
9. sedeō = I sit. A sedentary position is one in which one is sitting.
10. portō = I carry. If something is portable it can be carried.

Exercise 6.8

1. dormiō, dormīs, dormit, dormīmus, dormītis, dormiunt
2. veniam, veniēs, veniet, veniēmus, veniētis, venient
3. dormiēbam, dormiēbās, dormiēbat, dormiēbāmus, doemiēbātis, dormiēbant
4. vēnī, vēnistī, vēnit, vēnimus, vēnistis, vēnērunt

Exercise 6.9

1. The girl was not hearing the master.
2. The master warned the girl.
3. The girl was not hearing but was sleeping.
4. The master came towards the girl.

So you really want to learn Latin...

5. The girl gets/got up and walks/walked towards the master.
6. Her friends wait/waited for the girl.
7. The girl gave a big book to the master.
8. The wretched master fell (over).
9. The girl led her friends into the street.
10. The master slept under the table.

Exercise 6.10

The Romans were waging war against the Sabines. Tarpeia saw the Sabines but the Sabines did not hear the girl. The Sabines had big shields and beautiful bracelets. Tarpeia liked the bracelets and shouted. 'I like your bracelets and I will lead the Sabines into our town.' However the Sabines did not like the bad girl. They walked into the town and overcame the wretched girl with their shields.

Exercise 6.11

1. rēximus
2. surrēxērunt
3. cucurrit
4. scrīpsī
5. dūxistī
6. dēlēvit
7. sēdimus
8. timuērunt
9. mānsimus
10. dedit

Exercise 6.12

1. He/she has compelled
2. They have thrown*.
3. You (pl.) have sent
4. You (sing.) have fallen
5. He/she has ordered
6. You (sing.) have played
7. He/she has stood
8. We have written
9. He/she has given
10. They have conducted/waged

*For mixed conjugation verbs, see Chapter 7.

Exercise 6.13

1. He/she plays
2. He/she has played
3. We send
4. We have sent
5. We compel
6. We have compelled
7. He/she comes
8. He/she has come
9. We lead
10. We have led

Exercise 6.14

1. trāns + mittō = I send across. When you transmit something, you send it across the airwaves.
2. liber = book. A library houses books.
3. clāmō = I shout. A clamour is a shouting noise.

Book 1 Answers

4. regō = I rule. A regent rules.
5. surgō = I rise. To surge is to rise up.
6. re + surgō = I rise again. Jesus rose again at the resurrection.
7. scrībō = I write. A scribe is responsible for writing.
8. audiō = I hear. At an audition one is listened to.
9. dormiō = I sleep. One sleeps in a dormitory.
10. amīcus = friend. Amicable means friendly.

Exercise 6.15
1. Romulus was the first king of Rome. He ruled from 753-715.
2. He was enveloped in a cloud.
3. The Romans thought he had been taken up to heaven.
4. They gave him the name Quirinus.
5. Numa Pompilius succeeded Romulus. He ruled from 715-673.
6. Numa was best known for his building of the temple of Janus.
7. The doors of the temple of Janus were kept open while Rome was at war and were closed while she was at peace.
8. Egeria was a fortune-telling nymph to whom Numa turned for advice.
9. Tullus Hostilius succeeded Numa and ruled from 673-642.
10. Tullus spent most of his time at war with local tribes.
11. Ancus Martius succeeded Tullus and ruled from 642-617.
12. Ancus is said to have built the port of Ostia at the mouth of the Tiber.
13. Ostia was vital as a means of getting corn to Rome.
14. Tarquinius Priscus ruled after Ancus. He ruled from 616-579.
15. During the reign of Tarquinius Priscus, a slave boy was found sleeping in the palace with flames dancing around his head.
16. As a result of this incident Tullius was brought up as a prince and betrothed to the king's daughter.
17. As a result the sons of Ancus murdered Tarquinius Priscus.
18. After the murder of Tarquinius the slave boy became king. He was known as Servius Tullius.

So you really want to learn Latin...

CHAPTER 7

Exercise 7.1
1. cupiō, cupis, cupit, cupimus, cupitis, cupiunt
2. fugiam, fugiēs, fugiet, fugiēmus, fugiētis, fugient
3. faciēbam, faciēbās, faciēbat, faciēbāmus, faciēbātis, faciēbant

Exercise 7.2
1. 'Who has taken my book?' asked the boy.
2. 'We want to capture the big island' said the sailors.
3. 'Marcus' said the master. 'Why were you not hurrying?'
4. 'Who will lead Marcus to the fields?' asked the girl.

Exercise 7.3
1. puella parva ad Ītaliam nāvigābat.
2. ex oppidō fugere cupīvit.
3. 'quid facis?' inquit nauta.
4. 'ad Ītaliam' inquit puella 'venīre cupiō'.
5. tandem nauta puellam ad oppidum dūxit.
6. ad incolās miserōs vēnit.
7. 'cūr vēnistī?' inquiunt incolae miserī.
8. 'prope oppidum pulchrum vestrum' inquit 'habitāre cupiō'.

Exercise 7.4
After dinner, the girls were singing to the farmers. The son of the master wanted to hear the girls. 'Why are the girls singing?' he asked. 'Marcus,' said the master, 'the girls are singing about the woods of Italy.' 'What will they do after dinner?' asked Marcus. 'The girls will avoid the boys,' said the master 'and the slaves will drive the boys into the streets.'

Exercise 7.5
1. ūnus puer; puer prīmus
2. duo agricolae; agricola secundus
3. trēs nautae; nauta tertius
4. quattuor puellae; puella quārta
5. quīnque fēminae; fēmina quīnta
6. sex annī; annus sextus
7. septem Rōmānī; Rōmānus septimus
8. octo sagittae; sagitta octāva
9. novem tēla; tēlum nōnum
10. decem īnsulae; īnsula decima
11. ūndecim dominī; vīgintī dominī
12. duodecim mēnsae; centum mēnsae

Book 1 Answers

Exercise 7.6

1. VII
2. XI
3. XXX
4. XLIV
5. LXXXVIII

6. CL
7. CCC
8. DCCCXLV
9. CM (or DCCCC)
10. M

Exercise 7.7

1. 45
2. 254
3. 753
4. 1066
5. 52

6. 41
7. 61
8. 89
9. 2000
10. 1999

Exercise 7.8

1. octo = eight. An octet is a musical composition for eight players or voices.
2. quīntus = fifth. Quintuplets are five babies born together from the same mother.
3. duo = two. A duet is a musical composition for two players or voices.
4. novem = nine. November was the ninth month of the Roman year.
5. tertius = third. Tertiary means of the third order, e.g. tertiary education comes after primary and secondary.
6. quārtus = fourth. A quartet is a musical composition for four players or voices.
7. secundus = second. Secondary means of the second order (cf. tertiary above).
8. centum = one hundred. A century is one hundred of something, for example years or runs in cricket.
9. mīlle = one thousand; annus = year. A millennium is a period of one thousand years.
10. decem = ten. December was the tenth month of the Roman year.

Exercise 7.9

1. fīlius deī Rōmānōs regēbat.
2. Rōmānī dīs (or deīs) cantābant.
3. virī dōna deābus dedērunt / dabant.
4. vir bonus equum fīliīs et fīliābus dedit.
5. dī (or deī) incolās Troiae dē bellō monuērunt.

Exercise 7.10

1. The small son of the man hurried to the new town.
2. He avoided the farmers and led his horse to the daughter of the goddess.
3. The girl was singing to the gods near the walls of the town.
4. The boy wandered through the streets of the town.
5. At last he came out of the town and hurried into the woods.

So you really want to learn Latin...

Exercise 7.11
1. errō = I wander. An error is committed when one has wandered from the correct path.
2. novus = new. A novelty is something new.
3. capiō = I capture (or captīvus = a captive). A captive has been captured.
4. equus = horse. Equine means of or like a horse.
5. mūrus = wall. A mural is a wall painting.
6. vir = man. Virile means manly.
7. aperiō = I open. An aperture is an opening.
8. pellō = I drive; re (as a prefix) = back. To repel is to drive back.
9. faciō = I do or make. A fact is something which has been done.
10. audiō = I hear. An audition is a hearing, generally as some form of test for example for a musician or singer.

Exercise 7.12
Revision

Exercise 7.13
1. Servius Tullius was called Servius because he was born a slave.
2. Servius married his two daughters to the sons of the murdered king, Tarquinius.
3. The mild daughter married the hot-headed Lucius Tarquinius, while the hot-headed daughter married the mild Arruns Tarquinius. The girls were badly suited to their husbands and the marriages were thus failures.
4. Lucius Tarquinius was the hot-headed, ambitious son of the murdered king.

```
              Tarquinius Priscus
                    |               Servius Tullius
                    |             ┌──────┴──────┐
     Lucius Tarquinius, m. 1 = Tullia      2 = Tullia
```

5. Lucius Tarquinius sat in the king's chair and began to insult him. When the king arrived, Lucius threw him down the steps of the senate-house into the forum.
6. As Servius Tullius made his way home, Lucius Tarquinius's supporters murdered him.
7. As Tullia passed the body of her father, she drove over it with her chariot.
8. The scene of this crime was The Street of Crime.
9. Lucius Tarquinius ruled from 534 to 510.
10. He acquired the name Superbus due to his arrogance and pride.
11. When Lucius Tarquinius's son raped a girl named Lucretia, as a result of which the girl killed herself, the family of Lucretia drove the Tarquins out of Rome.
12. After 510 Rome was ruled as a republic. Supreme power lay with the two consuls who held office for one year and who were answerable to the senate.

Book 1 Answers

CHAPTER 8

Exercise 8.1

mīles	cōnsul	dux
mīles	cōnsul	dux
mīlitem	cōnsulem	ducem
mīlitis	cōnsulis	ducis
mīlitī	cōnsulī	ducī
mīlite	cōnsule	duce
mīlitēs	cōnsulēs	ducēs
mīlitēs	cōnsulēs	ducēs
mīlitēs	cōnsulēs	ducēs
mīlitum	cōnsulum	ducum
mīlitibus	cōnsulibus	ducibus
mīlitibus	cōnsulibus	ducibus

Exercise 8.2

1. rēgēs in urbe regēbant.
2. mīlitēs multa bella gerēbant.
3. urbem multīs sagittīs oppugnābimus.
4. cūr dux mīlitēs monuit?
5. Rōmānī ducem urbis cēpērunt.

Exercise 8.3

1. The king of the Romans warned the soldiers.
2. The soldiers led the leader to the city.
3. Romulus built a big city.
4. The soldiers attacked the city.
5. We overcame the soldiers near the city.

Exercise 8.4

flūmen	carmen	nōmen
flūmen	carmen	nōmen
flūmen	carmen	nōmen
flūminis	carminis	nōminis
flūminī	carminī	nōminī
flūmine	carmine	nōmine
flūmina	carmina	nōmina
flūmina	carmina	nōmina
flūmina	carmina	nōmina
flūminum	carminum	nōminum
flūminibus	carminibus	nōminibus
flūminibus	carminibus	nōminibus

So you really want to learn Latin...

Exercise 8.5

1. rēgēs bonī
2. rēx male
3. mīlitem fessum
4. flūminis parvī
5. operī novō
6. sine duce bonō
7. ad urbem magnam
8. sub ponte parvō
9. cum mīlitibus nostrīs
10. ducis īrātī

Exercise 8.6

1. Into the deep river
2. In the deep river
3. Near the big bridge
4. Against the tired soldiers
5. With the bad king
6. Down from the big tree
7. Before the beautiful song
8. Without a name
9. After death
10. Around the big city

Exercise 8.7

1. A bad king called Tarquinius terrified the Romans for a long time.
2. A girl called Lucretia feared the son of the proud king.
3. The soldiers of Brutus drove Tarquinius out of the city.
4. Tarquinius Superbus wanted help from a king called Porsenna.
5. 'We won't save our city, will we?' asked Brutus.
6. 'I shall overcome the enemy' replied Horatius 'and you will break the bridge.'

Exercise 8.8

Once upon a time a king called Tarquinius Superbus was terrifying the Romans. The king's son, Sextus Tarquinius, loved a beautiful girl. The girl feared the boy and shouted. However her friends did not hear. At last an angry soldier called Brutus overcame the proud king and drove him out of the city. The wretched Romans did not want kings and for a long time they had two consuls. One led the soldiers, the other ruled the city.

Exercise 8.9

1.		2.		3.	
hostis	hostēs	animal	animālia	pōns	pontēs
hostis	hostēs	animal	animālia	pōns	pontēs
hostem	hostēs	animal	animālia	pontem	pontēs
hostis	hostium	animālis	animālium	pontis	pontium
hostī	hostibus	animālī	animālibus	pontī	pontibus
hoste	hostibus	animālī	animālibus	ponte	pontibus
(Standard non-increasing)		(Increasing neuter noun in −al or −ar)		(Monosyllable with stem ending in two consonants)	

Book 1 Answers

4. fräter	frātrēs	5. urbs	urbēs
frāter	frātrēs	urbs	urbēs
frātrem	frātrēs	urbem	urbēs
frātris	frātrum	urbis	urbium
frātrī	frātribus	urbī	urbibus
frātre	frātribus	urbe	urbibus
(Member of the family!)		(Monosyllable with stem ending in two consonants)	

Exercise 8.10
1. hostēs pontēs et portās urbis parāvērunt.
2. Rōmānī hostēs ab urbe spectāvērunt.
3. urbem multīs sagittīs et tēlīs oppugnāvērunt.
4. dux hostium trāns pontem cucurrit.
5. Rōmānī mīlitem necāvērunt et corpus in urbem trāxērunt.

Exercise 8.11
Tarquinius Superbus Rōmam oppugnābat. cōpiās ad urbem dūcēbat. mīles Rōmānus, nōmine Horātius, trāns pontem festīnāvit. 'quid facis?' inquiunt Rōmānī. 'urbem nostram' inquit Horātius 'servābō. cum hostibus pugnābō et pontem frangētis.'

Exercise 8.12
1. cīvis = citizen. A civilian is someone who is engaged in civil (pertaining to the body of citizens) rather than military pursuits.
2. urbs = city. Urban relates to the city.
3. superbus = proud. Superb means very impressive or exalted.
4. altus = high. Altitude refers to height (above sea level).
5. hostis = enemy. Hostile means of an enemy or unfriendly.
6. arbor = tree. An arboretum is a botanical tree-garden.
7. māter = mother. Maternal means motherly.
8. pater = father. Paternal means fatherly.
9. iuvenis = young person. Juvenile means immature.
10. canis = dog. Canine relates to dogs.

Exercise 8.13
1. Tarquinius was not pleased because he had been expelled from Rome.
2. He sought help from Lars Porsenna, king of Clusium.
3. Lars Porsenna captured the Janiculum Hill.
4. The Etruscans were held up at the Pons Sublicius.

So you really want to learn Latin...

5.   Horatius Cocles resolved to prevent the enemy crossing the bridge.
6.   Horatius was aided by Spurius Lartius and Titus Herminius.
7.   When the bridge was about to collapse, Horatius sent his two companions back across the bridge to safety.
8.   When the bridge collapsed Horatius prayed to the river god, leapt into the river and swam to safety.
9.   Roman fathers used to tell this story to encourage their children to be brave and to put the interests of Rome above their own safety.
10. It is amazing how difficult pupils find this one! I would immediately think of David and Goliath, Robert the Bruce, General Custer, Nelson at Trafalgar, the charge of the Light Brigade...But such stories seem to have disappeared from the curriculum.

Book 1 Answers

CHAPTER 9

Exercise 9.1
1. Five girls and four boys were walking through the streets. They saw a bridge.
2. The girls were afraid of water and did not play near the river. Flavia however fell into the water.
3. An angry farmer called Sextus hurried towards the river. For he wanted to save the girl.
4. The boys and girls looked at the water. However they did not see Flavia.
5. At last however the girl's brother climbed down into the river and saved Flavia. For the boy loved Flavia.

Exercise 9.2
1. māter cōnsulis prope urbem manēbat. fīlius tamen discessit.
2. rēx mīlitēs ad flūmen dūxit. aquam enim ad castra portāre cupiēbat.
3. fīlia rēgis Rōmulum Remumque cēlābat. mīlitēs tamen puerōs in flūmen iēcērunt.
4. Rōmulus Remum necāvit urbemque prope flūmen aedificāvit.
5. Rōmānī pontem dēlēvērunt et ad urbem festīnāvērunt.

Exercise 9.3
Once there lived in Italy a big monster called Cacus. He used to wander through the fields and terrify the farmers. The inhabitants of Italy were afraid of the monster. For the monster breathed flames and had fierce eyes. At last a strong man called Hercules came to Italy. He had many bulls. When Cacus saw the bulls he dragged them into a cave by their tails. Hercules found the tracks of the bulls. However, he did not find the bulls. For the animals were walking backwards.

Suddenly one of the bulls shouted (roared). Hercules hurried to the place and wounded the monster with a spear. He killed Cacus and took back the bulls. Thus he saved the inhabitants from danger.

Exercise 9.4
1. The proud king terrified the Romans and did not love the city.
2. The father loved the boys but did not want to teach Marcus.
3. The girl wounded the master but did not overcome him.
4. The leader of the enemy was afraid of the Romans and was not leading his soldiers into Italy.
5. The inhabitants saw the sailors but were not overcoming them.

So you really want to learn Latin...

Exercise 9.5

1. et Rōmānī et barbarī pugnāre cōnstituērunt.
2. nec puerī nec puellae ascendere montem cupiēbant.
3. crās et montēs et flūmina vidēbis/vidēbitis.
4. nec dī nec deae virōs superbōs amābant.
5. ubi fīliī cōnsulis forum intrāvērunt neque audiēbant neque spectābant.

Exercise 9.6

Here are some suggestions:

1. They say. English: dictation, diction; French: dictée, dicter; Spanish: dictar, dicho; Italian: dichiarare, dichiarazione.
2. We shall climb. English: ascend, ascent; French: ascenseur, ascension; Spanish: ascendente, ascender; Italian: ascendente, ascensore.
3. Of the body. English: corpse, corporal; French: corps, corporel; Spanish: corpulento, corpiño; Italian: corpo, corporeo.
4. You were fleeing. English: refuge, fugitive; French: refuge, fugitif; Spanish: fugarse, fugaz; Italian: fugace, fuga.
5. To decide/set up. English: constitution, constitute; French: constitution, constituer; Spanish: constitución, constituir; Italian: costituzione, costituire.
6. Tomorrow. English: procrastinate, procrastination; Italian: procrastinare, procrastinatore.
7. Of the barbarians. English: barbarous, barbarian; French: barbare, barbarisme; Spanish: barbaridad, bárbaro; Italian: barbarico, barbarie.
8. The weapons. English: arms, armaments; French: armes, armement; Spanish: arma, armada; Italian: arma, armamento.
9. They will send. English: mission, missive; French: mission, missive; Spanish: misión, misionero; Italian: missione, missiva.
10. He/she has thrown. English: inject, project; French: injecter, projection; Spanish: inyectar, proyectar; Italian: iniettare, proiettare.

Exercise 9.7

Once upon a time a king called Minos ruled the island of Crete. The king held a great monster in a labyrinth. The monster often killed girls and boys. For the king drove inhabitants of Athens into the labyrinth.

A Greek king called Aegeus was ruling the inhabitants of Athens. The king's son, called Theseus, entered the labyrinth but did not fear the monster. He killed the monster and saved the inhabitants of Athens.

Book 1 Answers

Exercise 9.8

1. Lars Porsenna besieged the city of Rome with the result that the inhabitants ran out of food.
2. Gaius Mucius was a Roman patrician who planned to assassinate Lars Porsenna.
3. Gaius's plan went wrong when he killed the king's secretary instead of the king.
4. When challenged by the king, Gaius said that Roman citizens did not fear death. He added that there were many Romans who would risk their lives to kill him.
5. Lars Porsenna threatened to have Gaius thrown into the fire.
6. Gaius thrust his right hand into the flames to show that he was not afraid of the king.
7. Lars Porsenna was so impressed that he released Gaius and later made peace with the Romans.
8. Gaius came to be known as 'left-handed' because his right hand had been maimed in the flames.

Exercise 9.9

1. Without daughters
2. Down from the mountains
3. He/she has had
4. He/she has lived
5. They have come
6. He/she has remained
7. At last
8. The spears
9. You (sing.) will come
10. By way, by the road
11. We were calling
12. You (pl.) will rule

So you really want to learn Latin...

CHAPTER 10

Exercise 10.1
1. Mucius is a Roman soldier.
2. Tarquinius was a proud king.
3. Aeneas was the son of a goddess.
4. Now the river is deep.
5. Once there was a great city called Rome.
6. The goddess of wisdom was Minerva.
7. Once there was a beautiful woman.
8. We shall not be angry.
9. For a long time we shall not write; for we are tired.
10. The arrows of the soldiers were long.

Exercise 10.2
1. fessa est.
2. īrātī sumus.
3. agricolae superbī sunt.
4. erat puer nōmine Gāius.
5. num barbarī estis?
6. arborēs magnae sunt.
7. ubi sunt mīlitēs rēgis?
8. quis est dux incolārum?
9. crās fessa erit.
10. cūr iterum īrātus est magister?

Exercise 10.3
1. fuī
2. fuistī
3. fuit
4. fuimus
5. fuistis
6. fuērunt

Exercise 10.4
1. laetus est.
2. currit.
3. fessī sunt sed currunt.
4. agricolae miserī erant.
5. agricolās spectābāmus.

Book 1 Answers

Exercise 10.5

1. monuerō
    monueris
    monuerit
    monuerimus
    monueritis
    monuerint

2. rēxeram
    rēxerās
    rēxerat
    rēxerāmus
    rēxerātis
    rēxerant

3. ceciderō
    cecideris
    ceciderit
    ceciderimus
    cecideritis
    ceciderint

4. vēneram
    vēnerās
    vēnerat
    vēnerāmus
    vēnerātis
    vēnerant

Exercise 10. 6

1. The soldiers will soon have captured the camp.
2. The girls had wounded the boys.
3. The leader will have warned the slaves.
4. The sailors had seen the island.
5. The woman had not heard the boy's voice.

Exercise 10. 7

Gāius Mūcius mīles validus erat. mīlitēs autem Rōmānī dolōrem nōn timent. mīles ad castra hostium ambulāvit. servum prope mēnsam rēgis vīdit. 'rēgem gladiō meō necābō.' mīles gladium cēlāverat. 'cūr servum' inquit rēx 'necāvistī?' 'servus' inquiunt custōdēs 'rēx nōn erat.' 'mox mīles Rōmānus' inquit Mūcius 'rēgem necāverit.' 'in urbem tuam' inquit rēx 'veniam nec tamen cum Rōmānīs bellum geram.'

So you really want to learn Latin...

Exercise 10.8

1. **rogō** rogāre **rogāvī** **rogātum**
rogās rogāvisīī
rogat rogāvit
rogāmus rogāvimus
rogātis rogāvistis
rogant rogāvērunt

rogābō rogāverō
rogābis rogāveris
rogābit rogāverit
rogābimus rogāverimus
rogābitis rogāveritis
rogābunt rogāverint

rogābam rogāveram
rogābās rogāverās
rogābat rogāverat
rogābāmus rogāverāmus
rogābātis rogāverātis
rogābant rogāverant

2. **discō*** discere **didicī** -
discis didicisīī
discit didicit
discimus didicimus
discitis didicistis
discunt didicērunt

discam didicerō
discēs didiceris
discet didicerit
discēmus didicerimus
discētis didiceritis
discent didicerint

discēbam didiceram
discēbās didicerās
discēbat didicerat
discēbāmus didicerāmus
discēbātis didicerātis
discēbant didicerant

Book 1 Answers

38

Exercise 10.8 (*continued*)

3. **interficiō** **interficere**   **interfēcī** **interfectum**
   interficis   interfēcistī
   interficit   interfēcit
   interficimus   interfēcimus
   interficitis   interfēcistis
   interficiunt   interfēcērunt

   interficiam   interfēcerō
   interficiēs   interfēceris
   interficiet   interfēcerit
   interficiēmus   interfēcerimus
   interficiētis   interfēceritis
   interficient   interfēcerint

   interficiēbam   interfēceram
   interficiēbās   interfēcerās
   interficiēbat   interfēcerat
   interficiēbāmus   interfēcerāmus
   interficiēbātis   interfēcerātis
   interficiēbant   interfēcerant

4. **dō**   **dare**   **dedī**   **datum**
   dās   dedistī
   dat   dedit
   damus   dedimus
   datis   dedistis
   dant   dedērunt

   dabō   dederō
   dabis   dederis
   dabit   dederit
   dabimus   dederimus
   dabitis   dederitis
   dabunt   dederint

   dabam   dederam
   dabās   dederās
   dabat   dederat
   dabāmus   dederāmus
   dabātis   dederātis
   dabant   dederant

So you really want to learn Latin...

Exercise 10.8 (*continued*)

5. **veniō**   **venīre**   **vēnī**   **ventum**
   venīs   vēnistī
   venit   vēnit
   venīmus   vēnimus
   venītis   vēnistis
   veniunt   vēnērunt

   veniam   vēnerō
   veniēs   vēneris
   veniet   vēnerit
   veniēmus   vēnerimus
   veniētis   vēneritis
   venient   vēnerint

   veniēbam   vēneram
   veniēbās   vēnerās
   veniēbat   vēnerat
   veniēbāmus   vēnerāmus
   veniēbātis   vēnerātis
   veniēbant   vēnerant

6. **pellō**   **pellere**   **pepulī**   **pulsum**
   pellis   pepulistī
   pellit   pepulit
   pellimus   pepulimus
   pellitis   pepulistis
   pellunt   pepulērunt

   pellam   pepulerō
   pellēs   pepuleris
   pellet   pepulerit
   pellēmus   pepulerimus
   pellētis   pepuleritis
   pellent   pepulerint

   pellēbam   pepuleram
   pellēbās   pepulerās
   pellēbat   pepulerat
   pellēbāmus   pepulerāmus
   pellēbātis   pepulerātis
   pellēbant   pepulerant

Book 1 Answers

Exercise 10. 9

1.	He/she has risen	9.	They had come
2.	You (sing.) have driven	10.	They will want
3.	To hide	11.	They will have run
4.	I have departed	12.	He/she had sent
5.	You (pl.) have broken	13.	He/she has been
6.	He/she has adopted a plan	14.	He has learnt
7.	They have found	15.	He/she will go down
8.	You (sing.) have read	16.	They sit

Exercise 10.10

Once upon a time the enemy were fighting with the Roman forces. The soldiers fought for a long time but did not overcome. At last a boy called Mucius decided to kill the king. He hid a sword and walked into the camp. Then he killed the king's guard.

'Who are you' asked the angry king. 'Why have you killed my guard?'

'I am a Roman soldier' said Mucius 'and I do not fear pain.'

Exercise 10.11

1. bibō = I drink. To imbibe is to drink.
2. vōx = voice. Vocal is to do with the voice (e.g. vocal chords).
3. caput = head. To decapitate is to behead.
4. capiō = I take. To capture is to take.
5. dēbeō = I ought or owe. A debit entry on a set of accounts is an item which one owes.
6. dexter = right. Dexterity means manual or mental skill, from the idea of right-handedness!
7. dūcō = I lead. A duct is a channel which leads something somewhere.
8. ignis = fire. To ignite is to set on fire.
9. inter = between and rogō = I ask. To interrogate is to ask questions.
10. custōs = guard. If one is kept in custody, one is locked up and guarded.

Exercise 10.12

1. Over to you! See p. 94.
2. Cloelia and her friends demonstrated the virtue of bravery by risking their lives to escape from the enemy camp. The Romans then demonstrated the virtue of integrity by refusing to allow the truce to be broken.
3. Lars Porsenna could not cope with a race who were at once brave and honest.

So you really want to learn Latin...

4.   Model Roman qualities: pious (in the Roman sense, like Aeneas); resourceful (Romulus's plan for populating his city); brave in war (Horatius); brave in the face of pain (Mucius Scaevola); loyal (i.e. not like Tarpeia); virtuous (Lucretia unwilling to live after having been disgraced by the son of Tarquin); brave (Cloelia).

Exercise 10.13
1.   Something essential
2.   (An examination carried out) after death
3.   A great work
4.   In place of a parent
5.   Time flies
6.   (Proof that one was) elsewhere
7.   Hurry slowly
8.   Something written afterwards
9.   And the rest, and other things
10. Firm ground